MARK McGWIRE

MARK McGWIRE
HOME RUN KING

Jeff Savage

Lerner Publications Company ● Minneapolis

JB M1484sj

Library of Congress Cataloging-in-Publication Data

Savage, Jeff, 1961–
    Mark McGwire, home run king / Jeff Savage.
       p.   cm.
    Includes bibliographical references and index.
    Summary: Presents a biography of the St. Louis Cardinal slugger who broke Roger Maris' single-season home run record in 1998.
    ISBN 0–8225–3675–7 (hardcover : alk. paper)
    ISBN 0–8225–9845–0 (pbk : alk. paper)
    1. McGwire, Mark, 1963– —Juvenile literature. 2. Baseball players—United States—Biography—Juvenile literature.
[1. McGwire, Mark, 1963– . 2. Baseball players.] I. Title.
II. Title: Mark McGwire.
GV865.M396S28   1999
796.357'092—dc21
    [b]   98–43684

Manufactured in the United States of America
1 2 3 4 5 6 — JR — 03 02 01 00 99 98

Contents

Making History

Mark McGwire's lumberjack muscles shifted beneath his red and white Cardinals uniform as he strode to the plate, holding his 33-ounce bat of northern white ash as if it were a toothpick. The fans in St. Louis, Missouri, stomped and whooped and started Busch Stadium shaking on the bank of the Mississippi River. They had arrived three hours earlier to see Mighty Mac hit **batting practice** balls. With the game underway, fans wedged themselves into the aisles. Some crowded behind the screen, their hands and legs dangling through the fence. They had come to see if Mark could break the single-season home run record—the most famous mark in sports.

Roger Maris hit 61 home runs in 1961. Babe Ruth had set the record in 1927 by hitting 60 home runs in that season. When Maris was threatening to break Ruth's record 34 years later, many fans hated Maris.

Roger Maris hits home run No. 61 in 1961.

They didn't want him to break the Babe's record. They harassed Maris. Chasing the record took a heavy toll on Maris, but he was proud of finally breaking the record. The two numbers he asked to have engraved on his tombstone are not those of his birth and death, but 61 and '61.

Thirty-seven years later, deep in the summer of 1998, Maris's four children sat in the front row at Busch Stadium. One held a framed picture of their father, who had died in 1985. While rooting for Mark, they were remembering their father.

Mark had been on pace to break the record for months, but he wasn't alone. Sammy Sosa, a Chicago Cubs outfielder, was hot on Big Mac's heels. Sosa had 58 homers as he stood in rightfield when Mark came to the plate with 61 home runs.

America was gripped by baseball's summer of power. Forty special agents crouched among the fans in the outfield. They would surround and protect the person who caught the history-making ball, which was expected to be worth at least one million dollars.

Mark glared with piercing green eyes at the Cubs pitcher and dug his back foot into the dirt. Six feet and 5 inches tall, weighing 250 pounds, with 20-inch biceps and redwood thighs, he looked like Hercules in cleats. His red-whiskered goatee made him even more menacing. Mark had hit a lot of home runs, and he had hit them hard.

Mark had hit one out of Coors Field in Denver that landed in the players' parking lot. One shot had cleared the roof at Tiger Stadium in Detroit. He'd hit one out of Chicago's Wrigley Field that sailed over Waveland Avenue onto somebody's front porch. He had hit the longest home run ever at Busch Stadium. The 545-foot blast dented the scoreboard, which the Cardinals covered with a giant band-aid.

So is this freckle-faced, carrot top in a baseball uniform really Superman? Well, no, not really. He has 20/500 vision and can't read the big E on the eyechart without his contact lenses. He has terrible sinus problems, hates flying on airplanes, and is shy. He is sensitive and caring, cries at sad movies, and has a generous heart. He gives $1 million a year to care for abused children. He loves to watch *The Learning Channel.*

In the locker room before the game, Mark had held the bat Maris used to set his record. He touched it to his heart. Maris had hit his record-breaking homer in his home ballpark, in the fourth inning, with no one on base, 13 years after the record-holder, Ruth, had died. Mark went to the plate at his home park, in the fourth inning, with no one on base, 13 years after the record-holder, Maris, had died.

Mark tried to keep calm, even though he says he was "shaking a little bit, stomach turning, heart beating a thousand miles a minute." He crouched low and cocked his bat as thousands of cameras flashed around the park. His pigeon-toed stance, which had prompted one of his first professional coaches to say, "You'll never hit in the major leagues like that," still looked awkward.

The first pitch from Cubs pitcher Steve Trachsel came in, a low and outside fastball. Mark swung hard and connected. The ball jumped off his bat at 125 miles per hour—a low screamer to left. In the breathless second it sailed toward the wall, Mark headed toward first base. The 49,987 fans stared, wide-eyed and open-mouthed. Then the ball disappeared over the wall after traveling 341 feet for his shortest homer all season.

The stadium erupted in a deafening burst of noise. Mark pumped his right fist in the air as he set off on a joyous, sloppy trip around the bases.

Mark's record-breaking blast on September 8, 1998

Mark jumped into the arms of first base coach Dave McKay and—oops—missed first base. He flailed his arms and skipped back to touch the bag. Mark seemed to float the rest of the way, as fireworks exploded overhead. He shook hands with the Cubs infielders, bashed forearms with third base coach Rene Lachemann, and waved to his father and mother, John and Ginger, in the stands. "It's like we're in a movie," John said, "like we're dreaming."

Then Mighty Mac pointed to the sky in honor of Maris. "I don't remember anything I did," he said after the game. "I just hope I didn't act foolish." When he got to home plate, Mark gave his son, Matthew, a Cardinals batboy, a sky-high hug. Then he celebrated with his teammates, throwing his grizzly bear arms around everybody.

Mark waved and saluted to the crowd as Sosa came in from rightfield to congratulate him. Mark wrapped his arms around Sosa and hoisted him high into the air. Then Mark left the field and jumped into the stands to honor the family of the man whose record he had broken. Mark embraced the four Maris children and shared whispers with them. He climbed back onto the field and took a microphone.

Mark jumps for joy as he reaches first base and coach Dave McKay.

After he touched home plate, Mark gave his 10-year-old son, Matthew a big hug.

"I dedicate this home run to the whole city of St. Louis and all the fans here," he said. "Thank you for all your support. It's unbelievable. All my family, everybody, my son, Chicago Cubs, Sammy Sosa—it's unbelievable."

After St. Louis defeated the Cubs, 6–3, the Cardinals held a party on the field. The team gave Mark a 1962 Corvette, along with the baseball he had hit for the historic homer. A groundskeeper had picked up the ball from behind the wall. When the famous ball was presented to Mark, he immediately handed it to officials from the Baseball Hall of Fame. The ball, along with Mark's jersey and bat, are on display at the Hall of Fame in Cooperstown, New York.

Mark's mother, Ginger, and father, John, raised Mark and his four brothers in a happy and active household.

Destined to be a Gentleman

Mark McGwire was born October 1, 1963, the second of five sons born to John and Ginger McGwire. He grew up in the warm glow of the Southern California sunshine and a loving family. His parents taught him values that he would carry through childhood and into adult life. "His parents were so quality," said his friend, Randy Robertson. "Mark was destined to be a gentleman."

When Mark's father, John, was seven years old, he had gotten polio, a disease that attacks the central nervous system. In 1944, a polio vaccine was not yet available. John had to stay in a hospital for half a year. Even his mother couldn't visit him. Nurses would roll his bed to the window each day so he could wave to his mother on the sidewalk below. When John went home, his right leg was several inches shorter than his left. He did not let his disability stop him. He studied hard and became a dentist. He developed into a skilled boxer and golfer. In his 60s, he still rides a bicycle despite wearing a metal leg brace.

Mark's mother opened her home to everyone and shared all she had. "Mrs. McGwire was quite a warm and happy person," said Mark's Little League coach, Jack Helber. "She always had a smile on her face." Ginger's example influenced her sons. One morning when the family was late for church and Mark still wasn't dressed, his mother asked him, "Where are your shoes?" Mark looked down at his bare feet and said, "I gave 'em to Stan." Stan was his friend. "He needed 'em."

Mark and his brothers played many sports. Older brother Mike played high school soccer and golf. Bob starred for the Citrus Community College golf team. Dan was a football standout who later played quarterback for the Seattle Seahawks and Miami Dolphins in the National Football League. And Jay, the youngest, was a three-sport star in high school. Jay was perhaps the best athlete of all. "He was better than me," Mark said. But when Jay was 15, he was struck in the right eye by a BB that bounced off a tree, blinding him in that eye. With his impaired vision, he switched to bodybuilding.

Mark grew up in Claremont, east of Los Angeles, at the foot of the San Gabriel Mountains. He lived on Siena Court in a tan two-story house with brown trim and a tile roof. He decorated his upstairs bedroom with posters, pennants, helmets, and other sports knick-knacks. Mark didn't spend much time in his room, however. He liked to be outside in the middle of the action. Above the driveway was a basketball hoop for pickup games. In the garage was a full weight set and punching bag for workouts. In back was a swimming pool for water polo matches. Next to the pool was a golf green for putting contests.

Mark's childhood friends—Mike Murphy, Mark Stevens, Randy Robertson, Scott Larson, and Mike Green—often visited Mark's house. Mark's brothers and all their friends made the McGwire residence busier than a train station. "With all these boys everywhere, I don't know how Mrs. McGwire didn't go crazy," said Mark's friend, Randy.

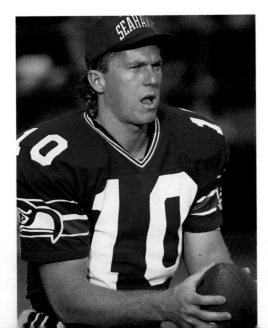

Mark's brother, Dan, played professional football for Seattle and Miami.

At Chaparral Elementary School, Mark's friends called him "Moogie." He paid attention in his classes and made good grades, mostly because his parents expected him to, but he cared more about playing at recess and lunch. He excelled at kickball and dodgeball. His favorite game was Danish, which has the same rules as baseball except the batter hits a tennis ball with his bare hand. Mark routinely smacked the ball over everyone's head.

Mark always liked baseball the best. When he was seven, he wanted to join a Little League team. His parents wouldn't let him. "I'd heard too much about arguing, meddling parents, and bad coaches," said his father. "I didn't want anybody to mess up my son. When I told him he couldn't play, he cried and cried and cried." The next year, John found a coach he liked and finally permitted Mark to play. Mark faced a 12-year-old pitcher in his first game. He hit a home run in his first **at bat.**

Tall for his age, Mark stood out as a pitcher, often whipping fastballs past the batters. But sometimes he couldn't seem to find the **strike zone.** One game, Mark walked so many batters in a row that he started crying on the mound. His father, who was the coach, told him to switch places with the shortstop. That's when Mark realized the problem. "I can still remember looking at the plate from shortstop, and everything was real fuzzy," he said. "I got glasses right after that."

Mark became his team's best hitter. By the time he was 10, he had developed a power stroke. He slammed 13 homers that season to break a Claremont Little League record. They weren't ordinary homers either. The three baseball fields at College Park were separated by a dirt area. Ordinary home runs over the fence landed in that open space. Some of Mark's homers soared beyond the dirt area and onto the next playing field.

In fifth and sixth grade, Mark also played for the school basketball team. He often led the Roadrunners in scoring and rebounding.

Mark took sports more seriously by the time he entered La Puerta Junior High School. He stood 6 feet 2 inches, and his friends called him "Tree." He pitched for the school's baseball team, played center for the basketball squad, and played quarterback and punted for the football team.

"He was the only intimidating guy we had on the football team," said his friend, Scott Larson. "When we came onto the field, we told him to look mean to try to intimidate the other team. He'd make this scowl, and inside we were cracking up, because Mark was the nicest guy you'd ever know. It was impossible for him to be mean."

Mark agrees that he wasn't mean, or much of a leader. "I was always the kind of kid who liked to sit in the back of the room and just blend in," he said.

Can you find Mark in this picture of his Little League team? He's the one wearing a red windbreaker and standing, the second one from the right. His friend, Randy Robertson, is the fourth from the right, kneeling.

Mark won plenty of trophies and awards, but instead of displaying them in his room, he hid them in the back of his closet.

At Claremont High School, Mark played freshman football in the fall. In one game, playing tight end, he caught three touchdown passes in the final five minutes. His pals Randy Robertson, quarterback, and Mark Stevens, running back, also played. Mark teamed up with his friends on the basketball court, too. But midway through the basketball season, he transferred to a rival high school, Damian High.

Damian was an all-boys private school with a distinguished basketball coach, Mike LeDuc. Mark and his parents thought Mark might learn more from Coach LeDuc. Mark hated to leave his friends at Claremont. At first he felt lonely and out of place at Damian, but he kept his emotions to himself. "We didn't talk about stuff like that in our house," he said. "You're never taught, these are how your feelings are. Anything like that, I always shoved inside."

Mark made new friends at Damian and grew to like his new school. He took college prep courses and practiced hard at basketball and baseball. In one memorable basketball game against his old school, Claremont led by three points with three seconds to go. Mark hit a jumper to cut the lead to one with one second left. Mark's friend Randy inbounded the ball for Claremont and a Damian player stole the pass and scored to win. "Hey, Randy, thanks a lot," Mark said kiddingly afterward. "We owe you one."

Mark remained friends with his old Claremont High pals, and they often got into mischief. One night, Mark and Randy were home alone at Mark's house when they heard tapping noises on the roof. "Listen, Mark, there it is again," Randy said, trying to scare Mark. Then Randy walked home. As soon as he came through his front door, the telephone rang. It was Mark. "Randy, there's someone in my house!" Mark said, "You gotta get over here quick! Bring your dad!" Randy and his father pulled up to the McGwire house to find Mark standing in the driveway, looking panicked. "Help! Help!" Mark cried. Randy's father stepped out of the car and called out, "Who's there?" Two boys came out from the garage. "It's just us," said Alan Ayers and Paul Brehaut, two of Mark's friends. "We were just tossing pebbles on the roof."

By Mark's sophomore year in baseball, he had reached his full height of 6 feet, 5 inches. Mark was an imposing figure on the mound. Batters feared standing in against his blazing fastball, which was clocked at 85 miles an hour. But when he got mononucleosis, a disease that saps a person's energy, Mark took a year off from baseball and joined the golf team.

The McGwires belonged to nearby Glendora Country Club. "Golf was the first game I learned," Mark said. "My dad taught me how to grip a club when I was five. I won some tournaments. The thing I liked about golf was that you were the only one there to blame when something went wrong. I missed baseball though, and I went back to it."

Mark's senior picture from Damian High School

Mark led the Damian High Spartans in hitting while setting several Baseline League pitching records. Coaches from Arizona State and the University of Southern California came to watch him play. So did scouts from major league baseball. Mark knew he would soon have to decide whether to go to college or join the minor leagues. "I was always just a basic athlete, nothing extraordinary," he said. "But I was a hard worker. And I liked to do a lot of that work where people couldn't see me. I would throw balls against a cement wall or set a ball on a tee and hit it." Mark's hard work was about to pay off.

Pro Prospect

Ginger McGwire never dreamed her son would be a major league baseball player, but she knew Mark dreamed of it. "As a boy, he'd lay on the floor watching baseball games on television," she said. "He wouldn't take the trash out as long as there was a game on. He always had that dream of playing in the major leagues."

Mark played two summers with the Claremont Post 78 Cardinals in the American Legion league. He pitched and played first base on defense, and batted **cleanup.** He blasted balls over the chain-link fence and beyond the evergreen trees so routinely that his teammates would hardly flinch. "He would hit these high popups that would go 400 feet," said catcher Matt Lumsden. "He hit so many of them it was no big deal. We just kind of expected it."

Mark and his teammates had the most fun on road trips. They sold Christmas trees to raise money to buy an old school bus, which they painted white with "Claremont Cardinals" across the sides. The first summer they traveled for three weeks through Nevada, Utah, Idaho, Montana, and Wyoming. They played in tournaments during the day and stayed in campgrounds at night. They slept on the bus, where most players could curl up in a seat. Mark was so tall that he had to put his head and shoulders on one seat and lay stretched across the aisle with his legs and feet on the opposite seat. He managed to get enough rest to strike out 65 batters and win six games on the trip, despite setting a record by hitting eight batters with pitches.

In Laramie, Wyoming, a college coach timed some of Mark's warm-up pitches with a radar gun. Some were going 91 miles an hour. The coach offered Mark a **scholarship** right on the spot. Mark respectfully said no. Mark's opponents in the far dugout were watching him, too. The father of a Claremont player wandered over to the opposing team's dugout. "Man, he sure throws hard, doesn't he?" the father asked. The players shook their heads nervously. The father said, "He's wild, though. He doesn't know where the ball is going. Last game, he hit three batters in the head." Mark threw a **no-hitter** that day.

The Cardinals took a similar trip the second summer but only got as far as Las Vegas when the bus broke down. Their first tournament game was in Utah the next morning, but fixing the bus would take a week. The temperature was 106 degrees, so a team meeting was held in a hotel pool. Mark spoke up. "My parents have a van," he said. "Maybe we can borrow it." Another player offered his family's station wagon. That night Mark's brother, Mike, pulled into town with the McGwires' van. The team reached Ogden, Utah, the next day, but not in time for their first game, which they had to forfeit. They won the tournament anyway. In 15 games across the western states, Mark batted .426 with 13 home runs and 50 **runs batted in.** He was ready to move up to the next level—college.

Two months earlier, Mark had met the baseball coach of the University of Southern California (USC) at a Dodgers game. Mark had signed a **letter of intent** to attend USC and play for Coach Rod Dedeaux. Mark was not yet sure he would play college ball, however.

Mark knew he would be picked in the June amateur baseball draft, when the major league teams take turns choosing players. Often the teams sign these players to contracts and then send them to play for their minor league teams. Mark loved the idea of playing in the minor leagues. Sure enough, the Montreal Expos drafted him in the eighth round and offered him a contract. He turned it down. "I really wanted to sign with the Expos, but the money had to be as much as a scholarship," he said. "And it wasn't."

So Mark went off to the University of Southern California. His freshman season, he hit just three home runs and finished with a **batting average** of just .200. He did win four games as a pitcher, posting a solid 3.04 **earned-run average,** but he wanted to excel at hitting, too. Mark decided to spend the summer playing for the Anchorage Glacier Pilots of the Alaskan Semipro League.

There, coaches Jim Dietz and Ron Vaughn changed the position of Mark's hands on the bat. What a difference that small change made! Mark hit .450 the first two weeks of that summer season. His swing had never felt better. But Mark missed Southern California. He fell into a terrible slump. Coach Dietz sat him down for a long talk. "He told me that I was going to have to deal with being away from home a lot if I wanted to play pro ball," Mark remembered. "What he said made sense." Mark started pounding the ball again. He finished the season with a league-leading .403 average, 13 home runs, and 53 RBIs.

Mark returned to USC filled with confidence. Gazing up at the locker room record board one day, he noticed the Trojan season home run record was 17. *That isn't really that many,* he thought. *I can hit more than that.* He told Coach Dedeaux he wanted to play first base every day so he could hit. "Sure, Mark, you'll hit more this year," the coach said, "but we still need you to pitch." In the seven games Mark started, he won three and lost just one. Mark posted the best earned-run average on the staff, even better than teammate Randy Johnson, who went on to win a Cy Young Award while playing for the Seattle Mariners.

Mark did some pitching for the USC baseball team but he really loved hitting.

At the plate, Mark blossomed. He batted .319 and knocked in 59 runs in 53 games. In a late-season game at the University of California at Berkeley, he hit a line drive to left that cleared the wall for his 18th home run of the season, breaking the school record. "Right when I hit it, I knew it had good enough height to get out," said Mark. He drilled another homer the next day to push his final total to 19. Mark's social life also picked up. He met and started dating Kathy Williamson, one of the USC batgirls. (Batgirls, like batboys, chase foul balls and retrieve bats during games.)

A college baseball player is not eligible for the amateur draft until age 21 or after his junior year. Mark knew his third season would be his last at USC. His teammates knew he would be drafted in the first round when the big contracts are offered.

Mark showed he was worth whatever money the pros would give him by clouting titanic home runs. He crushed one at Arizona State that sailed over the leftfield fence, over an orange grove, and beyond a street, before crashing to earth in a dry river bed. He hit one at USC that rifled into the parking lot with such force it caved in a car's windshield. He shattered his own single-season record with 32 home runs. He was an easy choice for First-Team All-America and was named *The Sporting News* Player of the Year. Then he said goodbye to the Trojans.

Next for Mark was the amateur draft. The New York Mets held the first pick of 1984, and they said they wanted to select Mark. They told him so the day before the draft when they sent team officials to his house with a contract offer. Mark said he would be proud to play for the Mets, but that he wished to wait until he was selected before negotiating a contract with them. The Mets drafted Shawn Abner instead. Mark was taken by the Oakland A's with the 10th pick. He was happy to stay in California.

Before Mark joined the A's farm system, he and Kathy Williamson were married. Then Mark joined Team USA and helped win a gold medal in Los Angeles at the 1984 Olympic Games. Finally, he reported to the A's Class A team in Modesto for the last two weeks of the season. (Class A is the first level of minor league ball.) In 16 games, he batted .200 with one home run.

Mark started the 1985 season at Modesto, and the A's were hoping to move him up to Class AA midway through the year. Those plans were spoiled when he started the year with a horrible slump. "I can't hit the baseball any more," he said to Kathy a month into the season. "I'm done. I've lost it. I've got to quit." Not only was Mark adjusting to the minor leagues, he was learning a new position—third base. The A's thought Rob Nelson would be their first baseman of the future, and they moved Mark to third base.

Like all good hitters, Mark kept battling and eventually broke free from his slump. He tore up the California League with Modesto, bashing 24 homers, 23 doubles, and earning the league's Rookie of the Year Award. He started the following season at Class AA Huntsville and hit 10 homers. When he moved up to Class AAA Tacoma, he hit 13 more.

Mark played for the Class AAA team in Tacoma for one season.

When the A's first moved Mark to the majors, they put him at third base.

Then, on August 20, 1986, the A's moved Mark to the major-league club in Oakland. Four days later, he got his first big-league hit when he singled off Tommy John at Yankee Stadium. The next day at Tiger Stadium, against Detroit's Walt Terrell, he belted his first home run. He got 53 at bats and hit three home runs before the season ended. But he struggled at third base and sometimes looked silly. In 18 games, he committed six **errors.** Still, the A's were determined to make him a third baseman. Mark had other ideas.

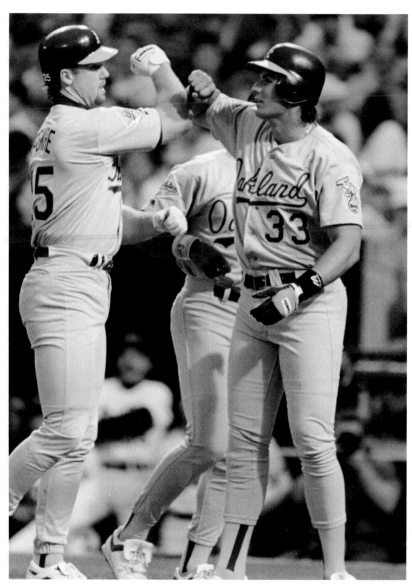

Mark and his "Bash Brother," Jose Canseco

Bash Brother

Mark opened his rookie year in 1987 at third base. He hit the ball so hard yet looked so clumsy in the field that something had to be done. Twenty games into the season, the A's scrapped their plans for Rob Nelson. They moved Mark to first base where he belonged.

In Detroit, Mark blasted five home runs in three days. In Cleveland, he went on another five-homer spree. By the **All-Star break,** he already had 33 home runs and 68 runs batted in. He was named to the American League All-Star team, which thrilled A's fans because the All-Star Game was played at the Oakland Coliseum. Although Mark went 0-for-3, they cheered him loudly.

The A's had another monster hitter named Jose Canseco. Mark and Jose celebrated hitting home runs by bashing their forearms, sort of like a massive high-five. They became known as the Bash Brothers.

No one had ever seen a rookie with Mark's power. In mid-August, he broke the rookie record of 38 home runs. Then he hit 12 more to finish the season with 49! He might have hit 50, but he skipped the last game of the year to be with Kathy, who was about to give birth. Mark's son, Matthew, was born October 4. "I'll never have another first child," Mark said, "but I will have another chance to hit 50 home runs."

Mark's 49 home runs led the league. He became only the second player in baseball history to be a unanimous choice for Rookie of the Year. He rejoined the A's for the 1988 season determined to win the American League Western Division title. As Canseco became the first major leaguer ever to hit 40 home runs and steal 40 bases in the same season, Mark was driving 32 balls over the fence and 99 runners home. Against the Boston Red Sox in the American League playoffs, Mark singled in the winning run to win Game 2. He homered for Oakland's first run in Game 3 as the A's swept the Sox four straight.

Reaching the World Series should have been Mark's dream come true. It wasn't. He was uncomfortable with the attention he got, and his marriage was suffering. To make matters worse, the A's were just about to win the first game of the World Series on Canseco's **grand slam** when Kirk Gibson hit a dramatic ninth-inning, two-out, two-strike, two-run home run to win it for the Los Angeles Dodgers.

Kathy and Mark have stayed friends.

Oakland lost Game 2 also. Mark still hadn't had a hit in the Series. In Game 3, he came to the plate in the ninth inning of a 1–1 tie. He blasted a fastball into the leftfield seats to win the game. "One of my greatest memories ever," he said.

It was the only hit he got in 17 at bats during the World Series, though, and the A's lost the next two games to end their season. Then Mark and Kathy divorced.

With Mark's personal troubles, he had to concentrate even harder to perform well on the field. He bashed 33 more homers in 1989 to lead the A's to another World Series, this time against the San Francisco Giants.

The A's won the first two games against their Bay-area rivals and appeared headed for success. But moments before Game 3, Northern California was rocked by an earthquake. Candlestick Park withstood the shaking, but homes and buildings around the Bay Area crumbled, freeways collapsed, and 62 people died. The World Series was delayed for a week. The A's won the next two games to finish the sweep, but the pleasure Mark felt in the championship was muted by the suffering and death.

In 1990, Mark led the A's to their third straight World Series. Along the way, he became the first player ever to hit 30 or more homers in each of his first four seasons. He also won his first Gold Glove for defensive excellence at first base. The Cincinnati Reds surprised the A's and swept the World Series. All Mark could say was, "We got smoked! There's no explanations, no excuses, nothing. They flat-out beat us!"

In April 1991, the Seattle Seahawks chose Dan McGwire in the first round of the National Football League draft. But as Mark proudly watched his brother join the professional sports ranks, his own career hit rock bottom. Mark lost his batting stroke. He tried changing his stance, his swing arc, everything to break out of it. He took advice from teammates, opposing players, even fans yelling pointers from the stands. "Keep your elbow in! Stand pigeon-toed!" Mark listened but nothing worked. Mark finished with a .201 batting average.

"I didn't like myself," he said. "I wasn't a very secure person. I was at a crossroads in my life." When the season ended, he drove to his home in Southern California. "I knew I had five hours by myself to think," he said. "I didn't turn the radio on, didn't play any music, nothing. I just thought. I was so down. I got to thinking about everything my father had been through. I mean, he never even got a chance to play baseball. I thought about Jay, too, how he had it taken away from him. I thought about how much I loved the game, and I just decided that there wasn't any room for pouting or complaining or anything but doing my best."

When he struggled at the plate, Mark changed his swing.

Mark's brother Jay had become a fitness trainer. He moved in with Mark to teach him strength-training techniques. Mark changed his diet and began taking bodybuilding powders and high-protein drinks. In six months, he added 20 pounds of bulk to his frame to boost his weight to 240 pounds.

In spring training, Mark worked with new A's batting coach Doug Radar to change his swing. He started using a low crouch and a slightly more open, quicker swing with no hitch, and a one-handed extension on the follow-through. Mark completed his transformation by growing a goatee. "I felt I really needed something," he said. "I think it's added about five years to my baby face."

Mark's baseball rebirth was complete. He roared to a flying start in 1992. On June 10, when he hit his 200th career homer, he was leading the league in **extra-base hits,** RBIs, **slugging percentage,** and home runs with 22. He was on a pace to hit 64.

On August 21, Mark had 38 homers, six more than anyone else. But that night at Oriole Park at Camden Yards, he strained a rib muscle. He missed the next 20 games. He returned in September to finish with 42 homers and a .268 batting average. He earned the Comeback Player of the Year award, but the rib injury was a hint of the trouble ahead.

For the next three years, injuries repeatedly disabled Mark. In that span, he played in little more than a season's worth of games. Critics blamed too much weightlifting for his lower back soreness and torn muscles in both heels. Mark said it was nothing more than bad luck.

When he did play, he was fantastic. He blasted five homers one day in 1995 in a doubleheader against the Boston Red Sox at Fenway Park. Oakland Manager Tony La Russa said, "He's so much better. He's better conditioned. His swing is quicker. He thinks all the time." If Mark could only stay healthy.

The 1996 season began badly. Mark missed the first 18 games with a foot injury. Then his fortune changed. When he joined the team in late April, he bashed home runs farther than he ever had before. He hit one 470 feet at Chicago's Comiskey Park. The next day he hit one 488 feet at Toronto's Skydome. He hit one 473 feet at Seattle's Kingdome, and on his next at bat hit one 481 feet. "It's hard to believe," said catcher Mike Piazza, "that Babe Ruth could have hit balls higher and longer than that!" Mark hit his 50th home run of the season and became just the 14th player ever to hit 50 or more in a season. He gave the 50th home run ball to his son, Matthew, and he finished the season with 52.

In the offseason, Mark met Ali Dickson, a woman who works at a home for abused children in California. Mark visited the home and met the children. Their stories disturbed him. As the weeks went by, the issue bothered him more and more. One day, driving past an elementary school, he pulled over and peered through the chain-link fence. "What kills me is that you know there are kids over there who are being abused or neglected at home, you just don't know which ones," said Mark. "And most of the adults who are doing it get away with it. It just breaks my heart."

The 1997 season for Mark was like a long home run ride. In April, he hit a blast at Tiger Stadium 514 feet—the longest of his career. The next week at

Cleveland's Jacobs Field, he hit one so hard it dented a scoreboard sign 485 feet away.

In June, Mark became the first player to hit two upper-deck shots at Florida's Pro Player Stadium. Two days later at the Kingdome, he hit a bomb off former USC teammate Randy Johnson that went 538 feet—the longest home run ever measured by a machine. He had 34 homers midway through the season and Roger Maris's record of 61 was in sight.

Then the rumors started. Mark would be a free agent at the end of the season, which meant he could sign with the team that offered him the most money. The A's knew they could not afford to keep him. They had to trade him to get something in return. But to what team? The Yankees offered cash. The Angels offered two players. The Braves and the Dodgers and other teams got involved. The uncertainty made Mark nervous, and he went 45 at bats without hitting a homer.

On July 31, Mark was driving across the Bay Bridge from San Francisco to Oakland when his agent called. He had just been traded to St. Louis. When Mark realized he would be reunited with Tony La Russa, who had joined the Cardinals a year earlier, he said, "Great!"

Mark said goodbye to his A's teammates, packed his belongings, and flew to Philadelphia the next morning. There he joined the Cardinals and played that night. The Cardinals played the next seven games on the road, and Mark didn't hit a home run in any of them. When the Cardinals returned to St. Louis and Busch Stadium, the fans greeted Mark with a standing ovation. Mark responded to the warm welcome with a 441-foot blast, the longest home run of the year at Busch. A few days later he hit another against the Mets. The day after that he hit two more. He had captured the city's heart.

Mark would still be a free agent at the end of the season. He had been making $9 million a year for the last five years. What could he get as a free agent going to the highest bidder? Fifteen million a year? Twenty million? "It blows my mind," Mark said, "that somebody gets paid that much money." Mark had fallen in love with the kind-hearted St. Louis fans, but he knew the Cardinals certainly could not offer him as much as the richer Yankees or Dodgers or Braves. "I'm just not going to worry about it," he said. "I'm going to do what's right for me. If it's not the going rate, so be it."

With two weeks left in the season, Mark surprised the baseball world by signing a contract extension, with a raise of just $500,000 a year, to stay a Cardinal for three more years. Two hours later, he celebrated by hitting a 517-foot homer against the Dodgers—the longest in Busch Stadium history. The next day, Mark said, "It makes me float every time I come to this ballpark, to play in this stadium, and play in front of these fans. I'm overwhelmed."

McGwire fans have sprouted up everywhere.

Mark had something else important to say. He announced that he was donating $1 million a year to abused children. A reporter asked him a question about child abuse. "Children are our future...," he started to say. Then he stopped talking. He opened his mouth but no words came out. He began to cry. "That day, when I cried, is when I realized I can open up. I can care. I can communicate," he said later. "It took crying for me to realize, this is the real me. I'm the Mark McGwire I'm supposed to be."

Mark finished the year with 58 home runs, joining Babe Ruth as one of the only two players ever to hit more than 50 homers in two straight years. The stage was set for his run at history.

Chasing History

The questions started before the season did. Could Mighty Mark McGwire break the single-season home run record? Could he pass Babe Ruth and Roger Maris? Could he hit 62? Mark wanted to avoid the spotlight and just play baseball. Instead, he had to stand still and answer the same questions over and over again. "I've always appreciated how difficult it is to hit 61," he would say. "It would have to be almost a perfect season for it to happen." Once in a while he would get so tired of all the talk he would blurt out, "How much more can you say about a home run?" Then he would calm down and say the familiar phrase: "The record is only in danger if someone has 50 before September."

From Opening Day in St. Louis, when Mark socked a grand slam, he seemed destined to break the record. He hit four homers in his first four games, tying Willie

Mays for the National League record. He hit 11 in April and 16 more in May. The only thing hotter than Mark McGwire on the baseball field was Mark McGwire in the stores. Across the country, fans rushed to buy anything with Mark's name or likeness on it. McGwire T-shirts, baseball caps, sweatshirts, plaques, coffee mugs, water bottles, practice jerseys and game jerseys. "I wish I had tons more of this stuff," said one store manager. "We just can't keep it in stock."

Mark hit home runs 28 and 29 at Chicago's Comiskey Park. "Mark hits it farther with less effort than anyone ever," said Manager La Russa. "You cannot put limits on what he can do. He might hit 40, 50, or 60 this year. He might hit 70."

Maris had been so nervous when he pursued Ruth's record that his hair fell out in clumps. Many fans booed him and even sent him death threats because they hated the thought of the Babe's record being broken. Mark felt something completely different. He received ovations on the road—for batting practice! "I wish every player could feel what I've felt in visiting ballparks," he said. "The receptions I've received—it's blown me away. It's absolutely remarkable."

Yet as Mark continued to hit them out...31... 32...33...the pressure grew. "It's going to be tougher for him as the year goes on," said career home run record-holder Hank Aaron. Two detectives protected Mark while the Cardinals were on the road.

Even Mark's batting practice draws a crowd.

Reporters, photographers, club officials, teammates, and opponents surrounded the batting practice cage. Mark complained that it had become a "circus" and that he felt like a "caged animal."

He hit homers 34 and 35 in Cleveland. "He's like the Empire State Building standing there with a bat in his hand," said Indians slugger Jim Thome. "Words can't describe how good he is." Mark hit No. 36 at Minnesota and No. 37 at home against the Royals.

"You're the eighth wonder of the world," Cardinals batting coach Dave Parker told him. "Aw, you're just saying that," Mark replied. He hit three against the Astros and two more against the Dodgers, including a 511-foot missile. "He's the one guy in baseball who could hit a ball that goes in one side of you and out the other," said Phillies pitcher Curt Schilling, "and it would be going just as fast when it came out."

Before a game in San Diego, Mark said, "I don't know how anybody can get used to this. I don't play the game for this. I'm sick of seeing my mug." Then he launched his 43rd home run. He hit No. 44 at Colorado and No. 45 at home against the Milwaukee Brewers. "I'm not doing anything different than I've been doing," Mark said. "People think that I just came in from outer space."

Cubs outfielder Sammy Sosa was slamming home runs, too. Sosa was two behind Mark when the Cubs and Cardinals met at Busch. They greeted one another on the field beforehand. Then Sosa hit his 44th homer to close within one. Mark answered with No. 46 to move back in front by two. Two days later, Sosa hit a pair at San Francisco to tie Big Mac. On August 19, the Cardinals came to Wrigley Field. In the fifth inning, Sosa slammed his 48th home run to move ahead of Mark. But Mighty Mac responded with one in the eighth and another in the 10th to win the game and reclaim the lead.

Then a reporter wrote that Mark used a muscle-building drug called androstenedione (an-dro-STEEN-die-own) in addition to other protein supplements and muscle strengtheners. Androstenedione, also known as andro, works like a steroid to speed the process of muscle repair. Mark said he used andro. "It's all natural!" Mark said. "This stuff is completely natural and legal!" He was right. Andro can be purchased in the store next to the aspirin and cough medicine. Although it's legal, some sports associations, such as the NFL and Olympics, ban its use. Others, like the National Basketball Association, allow it. While experts and fans debated the issue, Mark kept on swinging the bat.

He hit No. 50 on August 20 at Shea Stadium. Mark had become the first player to hit 50 or more home runs in three straight seasons. "That felt pretty cool," he said afterward. "I mean, you think of how many great home run hitters never once hit 50. Henry Aaron, great as he was, hit 47, what, one time?" Later that day, in the second game of a doubleheader, Mark hit No. 51.

Number 52 came two days later at Pittsburgh. No. 53 came the next day. Every morning newspaper put Mark's story on the front page and every evening news program started with a story about him. As McGwiremania swept the country, Mark spoke directly to young fans.

TAKING HORMONES:
WILL IT HELP OR HURT?

During Mark's chase of the home run record, a reporter saw a brown bottle marked "andro" among the body-building supplements in Mark's locker. "Andro" stands for androstenedione (an-dro-STEEN-die-own). What is andro?

Androstenedione is a hormone that is naturally produced in the body. It helps produce testosterone, which stimulates masculine characteristics. In this way, andro is like a steroid. In 1935, chemists figured out a way to make androstenedione. It is a legal drug that can be purchased in health food stores, so Mark's use of andro is legal. Whether it helps him is another question.

For years, some athletes have taken in more steroids than their bodies naturally produce in an effort to increase their muscle mass. Some steroids have been proven to help in the recovery and growth from exercise. There are side effects—such as hair loss, acne, and heart and liver damage—from steroids.

Androstenedione is not a steroid, but it may cause the body to produce more steroids than it normally would. Doctors don't agree on the effects of androstenedione although some studies have been done.

In the 1970s, some athletes used androstenedione in a nasal spray right before competing. They hoped it would improve their performance. Whether it did is uncertain, but it certainly did give them pounding headaches.

Sammy Sosa and Mark had a friendly rivalry in 1998.

"I know [athletes] are role models. And you may have a favorite baseball player," he said. "But how can that person be your hero? You don't even know him. Your hero should be your father, or your mother, or an aunt, or an uncle. Look to your family, to people around you."

Television shows like *The Tonight Show with Jay Leno, Late Night with David Letterman,* and *60 Minutes* asked Mark to be their guest. He said no. He didn't want to be distracted. Publishers and studios offered book deals and movie deals. No thanks, he said. How about a deal with McDonald's? "I don't eat Big Macs," he said. But Mark did make appearances for charities.

Mark hit a 509-foot shot against the Florida Marlins for No. 54. "I've never seen anyone like him," said longtime Cardinals great Stan Musial. Then Mark hit a 501-foot moonshot against the Braves for No. 55. "We don't say anything to him any more about home runs," said pitcher Todd Stottlemyre. "We can tell he doesn't want us to talk about it."

At Florida's Pro Player Park, Mark hit four homers in two days. On September 1, he ate an enormous plate of steak and chicken at a restaurant with his two detectives, then went to the field and blasted his 56th and 57th homers. He ate the same gigantic meal the next day and crushed No. 58 and No. 59 that night. "It's like *Star Wars* with Luke," Cardinals teammate Ron Gant said. "The force is with him." The following day was Mark's first day off in nearly a month. Instead of relaxing, Mark spent eight hours filming a public service announcement for abused children.

Mark returned with the Cardinals to St. Louis to find the Busch clubhouse filled with bouquets of red and white roses, stuffed animals, and other gifts. He shook his head in amazement. "The best fans in the country," he said. That night against the Reds, he hit No. 60.

Mark ate dinner with his family the following night. His father would turn 61 the next day. "Wouldn't it be something," Mark said of hitting number 61 on his father's 61st birthday. Everyone laughed. The next day, Matthew arrived in the dugout in the bottom of the first inning, just in time to see his father bat. Mark leaned over and kissed his son. "I love you," he said. Then he pulled his bat from the rack.

The fans at Busch stood hoping as Mark worked the **count** to a ball and a strike. Mike Morgan delivered a fastball and Mark slammed it deep to leftfield. The crowd erupted as Mark held his arms wide on his way to first. He pumped his fist as he circled the bases. As he touched home plate, he pointed to his father in the stands and yelled, "Happy Birthday, Dad!"

The following night, Mark hit No. 62—the record-breaker. Fans at major league ballparks around the country saw the historic blast on giant screens. At the U.S. Open tennis tournament in New York, large scoreboards flashed the news.

Word of Mark's accomplishment quickly traveled around the world. Thailand broadcast the home run in its midday newscast. Japanese newspapers ran front-page stories, and Japan's Prime Minister sent a congratulatory telegram. All of Europe heard the news almost as soon as it happened.

The season, and the great home run race, had not yet ended. Nearly three weeks still remained. Sammy Sosa had 58 when Mark broke the record. Then Sosa told Mark, "Don't get too far ahead of me." Maybe Mark listened. He didn't hit another for a week. Meanwhile, Sosa hit No. 59 . . . 60 . . . 61 . . . and 62. Suddenly Sosa and Mark were tied again.

Mark hit his 61st homer on his dad's birthday.

Mighty Mac responded with three homers to raise his total to 65. Sammy hit his 63rd, then he hit two in one day to tie Mark again. With three days left in the season, Sosa hit No. 66 at the Astrodome in Houston. Suddenly, Mark was trailing in the great race.

Mark didn't trail for long. Forty-five minutes later at Busch, Mark hit a blast to pull even again. Two week-end games remained in the dynamite duel. Then Mark exploded. He blasted two into the leftfield bleachers on Saturday, and bombed two more on Sunday. Sosa ended the regular season with 66. Mark had 70!

"This is a season I will never, ever forget, and I hope everybody in baseball never forgets," McGwire told the cheering crowd after the game. If his 70 homers were somehow strung together, they would measure 29,598 feet, a distance farther than Mount Everest is tall—and Mount Everest is the tallest mountain in the world. "It's absolutely amazing!" Mark said. "It blows me away!"

Mark could sit at his offseason home on the harbor in Huntington Beach and play a videotape of his momentous record-breaking home run. He could play it over and over again, if he wanted. But Mark doesn't even have a videotape of the event. He doesn't have any baseball souvenirs in his house. He doesn't have a trophy case. He has a pool table and a balcony that overlooks the sparkling blue marina where his boat is docked, but he doesn't have any framed jerseys on the wall or bats on display.

Mark has a place in baseball history, but he doesn't have much of an ego. He is a Gentleman Giant, a worthy owner of the greatest record in sports. "I hope my son grows up some day," said Mark, "and breaks the record."

Career Highlights

Minor Leagues

Year	Class	Team	Games	At Bats	Runs	Hits	2B	3B	HR	RBI	Batting Average
1984	A	Modesto	54	55	7	11	3	0	1	1	.200
1985	A	Modesto	58	489	95	134	23	3	24	106	.274
1986	AA	Huntsville	17	195	40	59	15	0	10	53	.303
1986	AAA	Tacoma	78	280	42	89	21	5	13	59	.318
Totals			207	1,019	184	293	62	8	48	219	.288

Major Leagues

Year	Team	Games	At Bats	Runs	Hits	2B	3B	HR	RBI	BB	Batting Average
1986	A's	18	53	10	10	1	0	3	9	4	.189
1987	A's	151	557	97	161	28	4	49	118	71	.289
1988	A's	155	550	87	143	22	1	32	99	76	.260
1989	A's	143	490	74	113	17	0	33	95	83	.231
1990	A's	156	523	87	123	16	0	39	108	110	.235
1991	A's	154	483	62	97	22	0	22	75	93	.201
1992	A's	139	467	87	125	22	0	42	104	90	.268
1993	A's	27	84	16	28	6	0	9	24	21	.333
1994	A's	47	135	26	34	3	0	9	25	37	.252
1995	A's	104	317	75	87	13	0	39	90	88	.274
1996	A's	130	423	104	132	21	0	52	113	116	.312
1997	A's	105	366	48	104	24	0	34	81	58	.284
1997	Cards	51	174	38	44	3	0	24	42	43	.253
1998	Cards	155	509	130	152	21	0	70	147	162	.299
Totals		1,535	5,131	941	1,353	219	5	457	1,130	1,052	.264

Honors
- Named College player of the year by *The Sporting News*, 1984
- Member of gold medal-winning U.S. Olympic baseball team
- American League Rookie of the Year, 1987
- American League Gold Glove, 1990
- American League All Star, 1987, 1988, 1989, 1990, 1991, 1992, 1995, 1996, 1997, 1998

Glossary

All-Star break: The four-day period in July when major league teams take a break for the annual All-Star Game.

at bats: Official attempts to hit a pitched ball. Hitting a sacrifice, being walked, or being hit by a pitch doesn't count as an at bat.

batting average: The number of hits a batter gets, divided by the batter's official at bats, carried to three decimal places. For example, if Mark gets 30 hits in 90 at bats, his batting average is .333.

batting practice: The time players spend before a game hitting pitches thrown by one of their own coaches.

cleanup: The fourth spot in the batting order. The first three batters are supposed to get on base so the number four hitter can "clean up" the bases by getting a hit that brings them in to score.

count: The number of balls and strikes against a batter. The number of balls is always given first. For example, if the umpire has called a strike on Mark but the pitcher has also thrown two balls to him, the count is 2-and-1—two balls and one strike.

earned-run average (ERA): The average number of earned runs a pitcher gives up per game. An earned run is a run that scores without the help of an error by the fielding team. To calculate a pitcher's ERA, divide the total number of earned runs scored against him or her by the total number of innings pitched. Then multiply that number by nine.

errors: Mistakes by a fielder that result in a batter or baserunner reaching a base safely.

extra-base hits: Hits on which a batter reaches second base or beyond.

grand slam: A home run hit with the bases loaded. A grand slam scores four runs.

letter of intent: A letter in which a high school athlete says which college he or she plans to attend.

no-hitter: A game in which the pitcher does not allow the opposing team a base hit over nine innings.

run batted in (RBI): A run that is scored as a result of a batter getting a hit or, if the bases are loaded, the batter drawing a walk.

scholarship: Money a college or organization gives a student to pay for his or her education. Colleges often award scholarships to students who are outstanding scholars, athletes, musicians, or leaders. Other scholarships are awarded by groups to students who have won contests, earned special honors, or demonstrated needs.

slugging percentage: A player's number of total bases reached on hits divided by his or her at bats. For example, let's say Mark gets 10 at bats in a two-game series. In those 10 at bats he hits 1 home run (4 total bases), 1 double (2 bases), and 2 singles (1 base each). Mark has 8 total bases. Divide that by 10, his at bats, and his slugging percentage is .800.

strike zone: The imaginary area directly above home plate between the batter's armpits and knees. A pitch that passes through this area is a strike.

Sources

Information for this book was obtained from the author's interviews with Jack Helber, Scott Larson, Matt Lumsden, and Randy Robertson and the following sources: Thomas Boswell *(The Washington Post,* 9 September 1998); John Cloud *(Time Canada,* 27 July 1998); Ron Fimrite *(Sports Illustrated,* 4 April 1988); Steve Grimley *(The Orange County Register,* 6 February 1984); Rick Hummel *(The Sporting News,* 1 June 1998); Richard Justice *(The Washington Post,* 8 September 1998); Tim Keown *(The San Francisco Chronicle,* 9 September 1998); Steve Kettman *(The San Francisco Chronicle,* 22 July 1998); Steve Marantz *(The Sporting News,* 14 July 1998); Michael Martinez *(The New York Times* 20 October 1990); Bob Mieszerski *(The Los Angeles Herald Examiner,* 5 May 1983); Rick Reilly *(Sports Illustrated,* 7 September 1998); Sid Robinson *(Pomona Progress Bulletin,* 13 May 1983); Claire Smith *(The New York Times,* 27 December 1997); Gary Smith *(Sports Illustrated,* 3 August 1998); Brad Stone *(Newsweek,* 6 July 1998); Tom Verducci *(Sports Illustrated,* 23 March 1998, 14 September 1998); Cynthia Vespereny *(St. Louis Business Journal,* 24 April 1998), and Steve Wulf *(Sports Illustrated,* 1 June 1992).

Index

Write to Mark

You can send mail to Mark at the address on the right. If you write a letter, don't get your hopes up too high. Mark and other athletes get lots of letters every day, and they aren't always able to answer them all.

Mark McGwire
c/o St. Louis Cardinals
250 Stadium Plaza
St. Louis, MO 63102

Acknowledgments

Photographs reproduced with permission of: Sportschrome East/West, Rob Tringali, Jr., p. 1; © ALLSPORT USA/Rick Stewart, p. 2; © ALLSPORT USA/Jed Jacobsohn, p. 6; UPI/Corbis-Bettmann, pp. 8, 37; Agence France Presse/Corbis-Bettmann, pp. 11, 53; © ALLSPORT USA/Elsa Hasch, pp. 12, 45; AP/Wide World Photos, pp. 13, 14, 34; © ALLSPORT USA/Ken Levine, p. 17; Seth Poppel Yearbook Archives, p. 23; Courtesy of the University of Southern California, pp. 24, 29; Courtesy of the Tacoma Rainiers Baseball Team, p. 32; Sportschrome East/West, p. 33; © ALLSPORT USA/ Otto Greule Jr., p. 40; © ALLSPORT USA/Jamie Squire, p. 46; © ALLSPORT USA/Stephen Dunn, p. 49; © ALLSPORT USA/ Vincent LaForet, pp. 56,61.

Front cover photograph by © ALLSPORT USA/Jed Jacobsohn.
Back cover photograph by © ALLSPORT USA/Brian Ball.
Artwork by Lejla Fazlic Omerovic.

About the Author

Jeff Savage is the author of more than 40 sports books for young readers, including Lerner's *Julie Foudy*, *Tiger Woods*, and *Eric Lindros*. A freelance writer, Jeff lives with his family in California.